═LETTERS═

TO MICHELANGELO

FROM WYOMING

LETTERS

TO MICHELANGELO
FROM WYOMING

BURT BRADLEY

WAYFARER
BOOKS

WAYFARER BOOKS

WWW.WAYFARERBOOKS.ORG

Quantity sales. Special discounts are available on quantity purchases by corporations, associations, bookstores, and others. For details, contact the publisher or visit wholesalers such as Ingram or Baker & Taylor.

All Rights Reserved
Published in 2021 by Wayfarer Books
Cover Design and Interior Design by Leslie M. Browning
ISBN: 978-1-953340-14-6
First Edition Trade Paperback

10 9 8 7 6 5 4 3 2 1

Look for our titles in paperback, ebook, and audiobook wherever books are sold. Wholesale offerings for retailers available through Ingram.

Homebound Publications, is committed to ecological stewardship. We greatly value the natural environment and invest in environmental conservation. For each book purchased in our online store we plant one tree.

CONTENTS

FLORENCE: CITY OF MICHELANGELO

ROME: THE ETERNAL CITY & CARAVAGGIO

MILAN: CITY OF LEONARDO

ARCETRI, FLORENCE: HOME OF GALILEO: THE LOST LETTERS

FLORENCE

CITY OF MICHELANGELO

ARNO, PONTE ALLE GRAZIE

Embarrassing sunset,
so damn cliché,
beautiful as a postcard
in this city of Michelangelo,
a pastel sky blushing
what's left of the florid
old river's ageless face.
Stretched flat and unwrinkled,
it moves by images of paint
and the blood of centuries:
red silt on its black floor.
Florence darkening like a planet
of old churches: its streets
like the river in no hurry
and beyond shame winding
through the old, narrow
shadows of night.

DECEMBER 14
Powell, WY

Caro Michelangelo,

Of all days, today, I thought of you. Not of your muscular heavens,
nor your giant glistening David, not even your smooth Jesus still
shining with death, the kind of death at which only a mother like Mary
can smile. Not <u>that</u> Pietá, but that last coupling, of mostly immaculate
rock, out of which rises the dead son carrying his mother who carries him
beyond her grief and your last days when there was nothing left, but....

And it is that great conjunction, coming not in the middle of your life,
but at the end, signaling yet another beginning. Like today, this morning
already rough with December, though not painful and not really numb.
This end of morning that began with nothing left, not even color.
Except one moment of stone sky chipped out of the dying air,
barely cloud, but enough.

Tuo Amico,
B.

DAVID, I

The giant boy poised, not posing,
his young old face shaped with beautiful doubt.
His Goliath side in feigned repose
of a seemingly careless youth idling
in the gargantuan shadow of Other.
His fearful sense of duty hidden
in the blessed rock supporting the tense thigh,
his flank of truth, veined with anticipation;
and the irony of his great muscled calf
stilling itself against the treeless stump,
mother source of holy marble and would be kings.

AUGUST 23
Powell, WY

Caro Michelangelo,

You know the most perfect things can become distorted
sometimes for the better, especially when it comes to what we
care about the most. Take a look at your David. God knows
he was nothing but a boy, a nice, small Jewish boy at that,
skinny and a little too sensitive (all that poetry and harp playing)
to be some kind of macho Samson with his jawbone of an ass
smiting everything in sight until hip-deep in Philistines.

But not Davy, who'd been most of his life a perfectly happy
kid, skinny-assed, naked skipping stones across the Jordan
at nothing, until the world wouldn't leave him alone.
It filled his head with Goliath sized ideas, all the old stuff:
power, money, sex, book contract for his life story,
so, he became huge with himself, you saw that
in his giant arms and hard thighs, his brow beginning
to wrinkle beyond any boyhood fancy, cold as marble
and calculating as his hidden rock.

Nothing like my son, a young man already, newly returned
home to Powell from college, because of the light and space here
of all things! He paints and doesn't care a fig about knocking them

dead as a great painter someday. I must admit he's a little on the soft
side, not much cold about him, though maybe a little hard headed,
but still boyishly lanky with a rather bad posture. And even if he liked
war, he would be a terrible soldier. Although he played a mean second
base, I'm afraid a sling-shot is out of his league.

But, sweet Jesus, he's as beautiful a boy as I could pray for,
with his brush sometimes dipped in water, other times oil, raining
colors onto his canvas, in ways that would pierce your heart, and
here in the middle of this godforsaken place, where he has found his
Goliath in huge, fierce, Wyoming. Sure, there are battles, sometimes
daily, yet nothing falls. And though occasionally things come to a
head, nothing is severed. Far from perfect, but in his own small
way, he seems to make everything grow larger, wilder. And I can't
find any fault in that.

Tuo Amico,
B.

DAVID, II

This the perfect man, *homo perfectus,*
with his disproportionate feet
and too large hands, the perfect
balance of his whole awkward stance
needing a tree stump to stop him
from falling over.

APRIL 28

McCullough Peaks, WY

Caro Michelangelo,

I know your first love is to sculpt, Carrara marble
in your veins. But there are no Davids, Moses, or Pietás here.
And yet, there is a Renaissance in this slow jumble of soft
sandstone, mostly dirt dried up beyond itself, caked into shapes
that resemble nothing in the world except ideal chaos.
And these works of art, maestro, are divinely devoid of anything
human, like these no name, poorest plants lying nearly flat
on the ground, cheaply leafed, not even cactus thorned,
haphazardly strewn like stricken lily pads floating across ponds
of shocked, brownless earth.

So why would I invite you here? Because it's spring,
officially for a month, and will be for maybe two months more,
which in Wyoming means winter hasn't entirely left. And summer?
Well, that's still anybody's guess. The sky here kaleidoscopes
in a constant metamorphosis of light and color and shape beyond
anyone's imagination, maybe even yours. And within these ungodly
peaks, you'll find the true genesis of the human spirit, this unearthly
earth, sun scoured, storm kissed, mottled green with clumps
of sagebrush scattered across a rough sea of cactus, tumbleweed, lava
rock, clay, and chert. And maestro, would you believe wild horses live
here, too? Skittish and rootless, they run alongside of antelope, coyote,

and rattlesnake—all who know where to find the trickster water, the sacred tough grass, the elusive shelter. This smallest of mountain ranges: treeless, unrestrained, ineluctable, a force unto itself.

And no one here but me with my back to a gritty hill, next to my son sketching shapes of light in this bulky space surrounded by the sheerest blue air. More precious than marble, these hills do not need a hammer or chisel, let alone shovel, pick, or ax. That sculpture already has been done by larger hands, greater tools. And yet, there is another way to consecrate this ground. I suggest you bring your brushes.

Tuo Amico,
B.

DAVID, III

The man carved of two moods,
yet not divided against himself:
knowing the illusion, he watches without watching
the giant world fall away, while grasping
the small hard truth, a momentary thing
almost without shape, yet real
in the capacity to dream.

LABOR DAY
Powell, WY

Caro Michelangelo,

A long life. Eighty-nine years, maestro, and did you ever think
of a vacation away from your breathing marble, your vital paint?
This holiday weekend, everyone else excited, thrilled! to be off
an entire day, three in a row of barbeques, beers, and boating
if they know someone with a boat, and then after the third sun sets
and the thought of work, of a job, of the grind, of necessity
begins to squeeze their throats. And then a week of suffocation
until the next Saturday, God, and Sunday too, when finally they are
safe, and off again. No Pietás for them, no Davids, no ceilings
of creation, their lives unsculpted, paintless, just blocks of existence,
colorless, utterly square, and shrunken, swallowed whole, unsavored,
unpreserved, bite-sized bits of death in life, chewed into
unconsciousness, ends in themselves, each a separate closed universe
that suffers from its own isolated entropy. And still, nothing done,
nothing felt, the life used up, the real work lost, the life forever off.
Forgive me maestro, so much waste has spilled me over. Grazie, for
sacrificing a moment away from your sacred labor to listen. I don't
believe in the Devil, but his boredom baffles me. Like you, my only
salvation is work now until I die at eighty-nine, or tomorrow.

Tuo Amico,
B.

DAVID, IV

Underneath his great feet, the tiny swarms
of ordinary humanity buzzing in disbelief,
while looking, looking, looking for a sign
and seeing none, no inscription, nothing writ
in stone or water, just the child's growth, the boy
beyond himself, becoming his own magnitude.
The crowd shuffles past on polished floors
like beaten Philistines, their ten thousand
tennis shoes in slow wonder
at the giant boy in his naked destiny.

We become aware, not of the myth,
or the obscure moral, but the little pulse
beneath our too thin flesh beating like a toy drum,
causing us to meander with the mark
of the futureless future on our furrowed brows.

What is it? This rock hidden
from our own Goliath nature?
We feel the need to be youth.
Yet our great and massive doubts
are equaled only by our hope
in the unpolished power of the child,

whose strength lies not in the throw
(that requires luck, timing, desire)
but in the secrecy of our faith,
though hidden in our grasp, tiny to us,
even less so to the world that believes
in the obvious, but a world nonetheless,
a kingdom in itself.

So, in our tennis shoes, poised
at our computers, we struggle with replicas
of the real thing to find our own providence
in the small, puzzling process.
And finally see, not what we know
or have come to expect,
but only what is to be seen,
here, now, not giant or giant killer,
just this chosen moment.

SPRING EQUINOX
Powell, WY

Caro Botticelli,

If you did landscapes, this would be your kind of day.
All innocent sky in an untilled field of clouds—lily shaped
and buttercupped, daisy round and petite for a while,
flirtatiously rolling in ringlets and curlicues all over the place,
landing nowhere for long, never far from the lengthening
gaze of the sun, and God! an utterly smooth eternity of blue
beyond the furthest idea of sky. If it wasn't for the armfuls
of wind, there would be no reason to breathe, yet breathing is all.
Though today is still too young and eager to feel supple or languorous,
its ungreen skin barely warm.

Undaunted, I planted myself in the middle of our garden
still dreaming seed and watched my youngest daughter, pink sapling
of joy inside a chubby coat, bouncing in half-leaps on short, unsteady legs,
so naturally tumbling in a small tumble and up again trying a circle
not fully round, but in stumbling spirals until dizzy and delighted
because nothing stops spinning like it's supposed to, and all this
with the skinniest notions of spring, mostly calf noises, bumpy twigs
and tiny crawling antennas over a toddler shoe of soft earth, thawing
where it's not supposed to, trickling mirrors of the vernal world to come.

Tuo Amico,
B.

AUTUMN EQUINOX
Polecat Bench, WY

Caro Botticelli,

Somehow, I don't think you ever experienced this
in your dear Florence. I'm overlooking these tough rocks
on this first day of the Fall. Just yesterday the last gasp
of summer fell down altogether with our first snow, brutally white
and severe as steel girders, the green life gone barren to the bone.
But today inside this orange rotund afternoon with pumpkin slabs
of light lying about, a bulging warmth already softening this gruff
earth until everything one last time glows cinnamon-leafed
in the corn sweet air. I swear, you would think some of your
cream-colored angels, or at least the kind of rough-cheeked
cherubs who hang out here, were conspiring to disturb
the death of Autumn.

Tuo Amico,
B.

JUNE 12

Hamilton, Alabama

Caro Botticelli,

I can think of no one else who used color
so vibrantly, with so much sensuality—God,
Spring's golden locks need no nudity,
or Venus, in clam pink hues and sunrise hair
that make the winds howl. Yet, here I am
in this colorless town that framed me so long ago.

      Not even this sunset, gone before anyone noticed
      (they're all driving too fast, lord knows where),
      though lavender and mauve, the last of it lingering
      in the small southern sky, almost hidden (hide and
      seek like cops and robbers?) behind a squad of pine:
      bars of rainbow light through a darkening forest.
      But nothing renaissance here—oh, bigger, more
      churches (one the shape of a bank) and a new jail,
      built again, not reborn from the thin, grayest air
      of this still, grape-less town. I know you can't help,
      except for me to know that somewhere in the world
      lives real color.

Tuo Amico,
B.

STILL LIFE IN A TUSCAN VINEYARD
(for John Giarrizzo)

Our backs to the wheel
of giant hay rolling nowhere
in the new middle of an old field,
just mowed and growing heat
in the slow yellow light:
our way of seeing Tuscany's
sweet red truth.

Here between the perfectly twisted rows
of newborn Chianti, seedless and still
too small: more flower than grape,
a long and slow summer away
from the blushing time of juice,
and years cool and dark before
the intoxicating moment
on wet, crimson lips.

For now, we watch the leafy sun
growing amongst the serene tangle
of vines, as we sit in the shrinking coolness
of the great roll of hay,
our little yellow planet,
whose unhurrying shade rounds
our sense of ripening.

GOOD FRIDAY

Powell, Wyoming

Caro Cellini,

You know I have never really wanted to write you.
I'm not certain why. Fear maybe. Maybe a bit of loathing.
After that time in Florence when the Uffizi was bombed,
your Perseus outside unharmed with his swollen sword in one hand,
the other clutching the old woman's snake-infested head, and
his cool "look what I did" demeanor thrust into the shocked air.
That was enough, though I read parts of your autobiography:
the artist of swagger, bravado, and contempt against the world,
bronzed like a beetle in your own hard-shelled ego. But you
worked and worked and worked until beyond your own sense
of self, and that may be your salvation. Maybe that's why
about five-thirty this morning I thought of you.

This huge storm leapt out of a soft midnight, unmolded,
castless, clayless, nothing but a roaring shape. Its black wind so deep,
so much blackness itself, I swear it was like some kind of obsidian
apocalypse (if I believed in Hell, this would have been it).
It was inconceivable, given that just yesterday trembled timidly
beneath a maternal light, the world curious and naive
with soft, sucking sounds, pale sprouts of lavender flowers,
and the smallest crawling life. Even some people I met
were turning green again, pastoral with fairytale grins on their faces.
A few of the more lion-like already willing to lie down, be fleece,
or follow some unseen, unheard bell with a new-found belief

19

in the well-worn Passion. But at dawn, despite this gnashing welter
of something too fierce, severing the world from itself, there is,
a kind of beauty to it. Signore, you may well laugh.

For even as the bloody sky begins its blood-letting,
there rolling painlessly across the sidewalk, silly and slow,
one of those little gray "sow bugs" feeling its way around
and over the bits of dead debris. Stumped a moment (never
by the storm) because of a gum wrapper stuck whistling in a crack,
it backs up, turns left and then right again and unwaveringly
onward to the still vague lawn hinting something green,
having grown out of nothing only the day before. It will probably
take him to Easter when this storm may be, at best, a memory
of misdirection.

What does it mean? I don't know, except I'd skip
the Sunday mass at the Duomo, if I were you. Head for Rome
instead. The Santa Maria del Popolo. You know that old, dark
Franciscan church, austere, drafty, damn near dead, but
a resurrection in itself. That's where you will find Caravaggio's
upside-down Peter and flat-on-his-back Paul—both aimed at
Heaven, all the way from the earth's heroic floor.

Tuo Amico,

B.

PIAZZA DELLA SIGNORIA, AFTER THE BOMB

On this softest June evening,
the piazza quivers,
nervous as a small animal
under the glare of spotlights.
This silence, a loud hint:
something happened here.

Glistening around the edges of the square,
the carabinieri, bullet-eyed, peer out
from the metallic shadows thick
and shiny with their small black cars.

They watch the crowd in a pantomime
of strolling promenade by the new chain-link
fence, pseudo silver and silly looking
under the portable stadium lights.

Behind it, a defenseless Perseus
lifts the old woman's writhing head,
an act, at least, that needs no translation,
his rusted sword unable to scratch
the heavily armed night.

CELLINI'S PERSEUS,
(A Week After the Bombing of the Uffizi)

Only fifty feet from his great blackened foot,
black as the witch's head he's holding
up in the still nervous air. I suppose
he began in some kind of bronze glory,
dazzled by dreams of where he was going,
what he might do, maybe even who he was.
And then all that time out in the world
somehow darkened the green life in him,
the boyish hue discoloring from envy
of the hero he wasn't, the hero he didn't have to be.

Maybe if he wouldn't have promised so much,
no one would've given him the sword,
and he would have left the ugly woman alone
to grow old gracefully: maybe cut her hair,
shedding her monstrous vanity, or keep it
long, but modestly tied in a bun,
letting it down only at night, spilling
harmlessly from her quiet head onto
the smooth undisturbed pillow next to her.

Maybe then he would have softened
with time, become something else,

something less violent, more heroic:
a swordless gardener on his quest for vegetables,
Cellini casting a trowel in a bloodless hand,
and a leafy head of lettuce held high
in the other hand of the green triumph.

Maybe then four hundred and fifty years
and last week would have been whole,
shaped only by an explosion of spring flowers,
spilling red only as chianti, or the appled cheeks
of children ringing around unanxious roses.

OLD FLORENCE

Hard to believe, *trattoria* after *trattoria*,
shop after shop, bar after bar,
the menu in English, the prices in dollars,
In the Piazza Santa Croce just beneath the gleaming
rough statue of Dante's stony gaze,
the great church behind him, a monstrous icon
to the vanity of old Florence, I stare
at the fleshless faces of both
and find the spirit in them unmade.

An old Florentine, old beyond reason,
his old bent bones crazy walking by Dante
past the church steps, without a thought
of going in, because of all his yelling
at the boys who have teased him beyond himself,
three or four of them on bikes, staying far
enough away from his toothless rage,
dancing about in their unwrinkled youth
yet close enough to be baptized with him
in the glaring shadow of the church.

He stumbles out first, like a drowning man
across the waterless piazza, flaying
his boney arms loudly in the dark air,

spitting out curses at the boys already
in the shadows having lost interest,
at the cloudless sky and stone-deaf Dante,
at the helpless old church becoming hoarse
and finally silent as old Florence having lost
his voice, last source of his undying vanity.

OCTOBER 22
Badger Basin, WY

Caro Dante,

I don't know how the Japanese do it.
Imagine saying it all in three lines!
Of course, you understood. Your huge

largely humorless comedy piled into pages
from hell to heaven, but only understood
bit by bit, ye olde three lines at a time,

dazzling pieces of the divine mirror.
As I sit here beyond good and evil,
on an alkaline hill, caked, cracked,

a chalky lump of rootless dirt, where not even
any dreadful, needled cactus or sagebrush
or something called skunkweed grows

under the empty sky going grey and vague
with a scattering of shapeless clouds,
loose and blank as a thousand pages

of an unwritten epic about this godforsaken world:
three lines hell, too abstract for the Japanese,
this koan Wyoming.

Tuo Amico,
B.

February 11

Badger Basin, WY

Caro Dante,

Out here further than most
have ever been I'm sure. Because
it is so harsh, so inhuman, the last
water (and Sand Coulee's hardly big
enough for a ferryman) was two or three
torturous miles back. If anybody could imagine,
I guess only you could—yet even this "hell"
would freeze your great imagination.
This is the tenth circle below that fetid ice
where your foul, old devil sits stuck
crunching his enemy's traitors—beyond that,
believe me, Satan himself, for all his tropical passions
would, like the plague, avoid this place. Especially
today, ten degrees from zero and falling still
with a pitiful sun, here where the deadest
metaphors for liquid lie in the volcanic
coagulation of sandstone, brushless sagebrush,
and fossilized gullies of some long, forgotten flood.
The very dirt itself, just so much frozen dust,
so dry, so cold, it must be the furthest damned

thing in God's creation, so the only Comedy
here is the utterly divine absence of souls.

Tuo Amico,
B.

ROME

THE ETERNAL CITY & CARAVAGGIO

ROMAN BEAUTY
(Piazza Navona)

Out of the enveloping night,
chiaroscuro and mythical,
she moves, essence of all that is
provocative in Rome, and still

moving into the fountain's sphere,
while the crowd swirls about
her lithe obstruction, olive eyed
with hair like tapered smoke.

For the first time, Bernini's boys
frozen stiff, beneath the swollen moon
drifting behind a canvas of clouds.

From their tombs, Leonardo
da Vinci and Michelangelo,
Botticelli and Raphael rise to reach
for their brushes.

OCTOBER 1

Kelley, WY

Caro Michelangelo,

Man, I don't know how, but I got lost today: the words,
the world all knotted up. I couldn't see where I was going,
how to proceed, or what it is I am supposed to focus on.
I wanted to write about everything, but what first? I doubt
if it was a problem for you. God, Adam, David, Mary,
and every angel in the Christian pantheon, there was an ideal
everywhere to be conceived in paint, born of stone. Never all
at once, never in a day, but brush stroke by brush stroke, hammer
chink by chink by chink.

I can't believe I'm here before one of the world's altars,
the pristine Tetons, huge and magnificent, crowned with clouds,
bleeding light with a jagged visage that reminds me of your horned
Moses, as if lightning became rock, or was birthed from it. Yet,
I stood before them without a word of homage. Worse, I was
drowning in autumn's ecstasy of color, its great flaxen surge of light
like the sun smashing into the earth scattering itself across
the ground, trees aflame, roaring saffron, chartreuse, with scales
of dragon gold, the leaves spangling so bright becoming their own light. You
could see them one at a time, each meticulously veined, splintered, toothed,
leaf by miraculous leaf.

Maybe that's it? It's not enough to paint creation on the ceiling,
but the floor, too, and the walls, the doors, spilling onto the porch, up
on the roof—God, the very air, and raining down on every stone, wet
glistening, each a shape of eternity, of generation, of angelic color.

I ran outside into what was left of the night. I was reaching I know,
but I reached out for anything and picked up a rock from the black
earth. I held its smooth, muddy weight not quite round in my palm.
Inside under the lamp, I saw it was slate blue, mottled with white spots
and chipped on one side as if it was part of something bigger.
Slowly, I understood that like David or Moses or the Pietá, it was
the presence of rock, one rock, all rock, present as any pulse beneath
my skin. And like some kind of household God, its unadorned spirit,
naked yet opaque, unto itself, reveals nothing unnecessary, only
its singularity (for a single moment).

And so, it is in one hue, one crystalline point of time, when the sky,
the world, and a piece of granite are themselves, understood. And
that nothing comes first, no hierarchy of perceptions, of process.
This then, I realized was the source of my chaos, and the way,
finally, out of it: what you knew all your life, that there is only
the doing. And out of that everything else follows.

Tuo Amico,
B.

DECEMBER 22

Powell, WY

Caro Caravaggio,

Today started so dark you would have thought somehow
night was happening. Autumn, after having hung on by its knuckles,
fleshless bone and pale, but never bitter, fell for good. And now
winter as cold as old stone and something of that old dark
Franciscan church, Santa Maria del Popolo, where your *Crucifixion
of Peter* faces your *Conversion on the Way to Damascus*, where
the Franciscan monks there must like their angels the way you
and I do—muscular or voluptuous, even freckled, skin like birch bark,
wings full of twigs and debris, mouths smelling of cracked hazelnuts
and flaming dawn hair like my daughter's, who is all earth running,
running, everywhere room to room just ahead of her laughing and her
"you can't catch me," with cinnamon in her voice, the joy of the now
in her eyes.

Yet there she was having dragged the coffee table book of your work—
prints only 10" x 14"; God, your triptych shrunken to a television screen,
but not for her, my live cherub descending upon the color plates
like they were Eden before the Fall—and every one she wants me to say
who's that, her fingers on Matthew, on Bacchus, on *Mary in Death
of a Virgin* ("Daddy why's she sleeping?").

But it's the beheaded Medusa, shocked in her new severance, her hair
still writing, and *Judith Beheading Holofernes* (I couldn't turn the page
fast enough) and the blasé boy David holding the astonished head
of Goliath to whom this dove-like child of mine is so drawn:
to these unlit souls so recently cut off from their heartless hearts.
Is it that she must acquaint herself with the aesthetics of the
grotesque in order to know that the truth of beauty lies
not simply in the paint but that it is also the selfless
heart (not the self-righteous ego) that understands
out of destruction comes creation.

Tuo Amico,
B.

CHRISTMAS

Powell, Wyoming

Caro Caravaggio,

Winter's white-smocked and mostly mute today. No promises
of something better to come. Just this stone quiet prayer,
not to anyone, for anything, not even to continue—praying
a deep tableau of blessed cold. Like the hollow cheek of your Jesus,
his long-curved finger pointing to the bald disbelief of St. Matthew.
He's a ruddy-faced savior, I swear, and from ten feet away in the cold
Church of San Luigi dei Francesi I could see the pockmarks
of your hope for someone real who felt something worth doing,
every day, without fanfare and talking about it. Like here today
in Powell, bright as a corpse and thin as Jesus' wrist, a calling in
itself when the sleeves of its robe are rolled up loudly in this month
of red faith.

Tuo Amico,
B.

MARCH 6

Powell, WY

Caro Caravaggio,

Damn, can you believe it? On Michelangelo's
birthday, I think I understand what you knew about
chiaroscuro. It was a little after four this morning here,
just after a hell of a snowstorm that began in the middle
of a lifetime ago, and really got deep after the dying sun died
for good, though when that was no one could say. So unbelievably
white everywhere in the utter blackness, a time for dream,
but my youngest needed her medicine, so neither of us slept
through the sick, dark, cold. Still, there was a window,
so I looked. And amongst all the piles of storm where the earth
and animals used to be, in a pristine clearing where the wind
seemed to lose its breath, and random bits of light lay scattered
over the unbelievable emptiness, I had this vision of sorts,
barely awake, of all color collapsed, when absence happens,
and colorless, without character, a perfect shape is born
still without shell, bone, or sap in the liquid center of dust
to dust, no matter how real the dark, everything is purely
light, light, light.

Tuo Amico,
B.

MAY 18
Timber Creek, WY

Caro Caravaggio,

Man, it is hard to believe it has already been almost
a year since we prayed at your "altar" in the San Luigi dei Francesi.
The Matthew triptych, God! where we watched for hours
the revelations of holy chiaroscuro, the Christ red robes,
and surreal gestures of an angel's hands.

Now here, oh the joy of this new before-I-was-born feeling
of being in the mountains. First, the fifty-mile drive to Meeteetsee—
a Shoshone name that has lost its original meaning. However, in this
town born of the old West, it means a couple of cowboy bars—
Elkhorn's my favorite—one school (grades k-12), a church or two,
and a strange motel called Vision Quest all-in three-square miles.
Once through, I headed for the Pitchfork Ranch and Sunshine
Reservoir. Both the wrong way for different reasons. The latter
because it is not far enough, and the ranch being too far. But
somewhere between I turn due south to Timber Creek onto a mud
rutted road threatening at the first big rain to become something more
terrible and less defined.

But clearly the drive was worth it. I arrive at a meadow in the middle
of heaven on earth where a lot of the quiet life is left undisturbed, and

even allowed to make its own kind of noise: Redtail arias of hawk and raven, the creek singing silt, with mosquito martins, woodpecker wood meditations and young aspens practicing their green airs.

To sleep not needing to dream, I listen to songs of the earth
for the sun that died every night: wind elegies sung through
the choruses of spruce and pine after hymns of nothing but the gray
whispers of thin clouds that never amounted to much during the day.
Finally, silence falling like the light in your triptych from a wine dark
heaven only to erupt in a percussion of cobalt thunder and alabaster
zigzags of lightning. God, to see you again here in Rome,
what a joy to contemplate.

Tuo Amico,
B.

On Caravaggio's John the Baptist

He's poised, so much more light
than is possible for such brooding,
such knowledge—not sitting,
not resting, but taut, half
leaning—wounded perhaps,
unable to stand yet refusing to slump.
He is the shape of recognition
of what one must do,
even his darkness is brilliant.

The face with its raccoon mask,
a thief with no need to steal,
a blind man with no eyes to see,
the blackness is enough.
Like a bell ringer, he hangs
onto his bamboo staff,
with its crucifix lost in the falling
of unearthly browned leaves.

But there is nothing to fall
back on, except the fringed blood
of cloth, flung like a red wind
about him. There is evidence

of the battle just won or lost or to be:
the bright knee scraped to rose,
that blackened toe nail (there
is no leaving anything behind)
and the hand! with its desert rouge
roughened fingers, yet a bright grasp
of the reed staff, an earthen hand
in need of Jordan's baptismal water.

JULY 7
Powell, WY

Caro Caravaggio,

You'll laugh, but my daughter, only three years old
and already acknowledging you as the master, today began
painting with watercolors (her medium, I guess),
dipping her brush into the black, (you know, of course,
the possibilities of that pigment), a rainbow she murmurs
and continues to mine the little black well. At first a blotch
on the calm whiteness, then at least forty swellings
and forty heavings to a great flood of black sky, threatening
more than rain, and blacker still—there's no rest during creation,
only genesis over and over again. The brush is not enough,
so fingers begin brooding upon the deep, and the black begets
blue and blue begets purple that begets red that begets green
and the page becomes abandoned for the table, for infinite space
and a fixed idea under her tiny trickster hands stained
with imagination, black beyond blackness, the color of joy.

Tuo Amico,

B.

August 5

Heart Mountain, WY

Caro Caravaggio,

My father has come and gone. Drove in from California,
stayed three days and left. He's a fighter you know;
not just former middle-weight champ of the army, but a fire fighter
for thirty years, not to mention he's been fighting the American
Dream all his life. I'm not sure for or against, but dreams bother him
as much as the everyday stuff. So, he's never given much credence
to the arts. Poetry, painting, even music, he's never thought enough
of to fight, much less embrace. I mentioned your name, your work,
comparing your paint to Michelangelo's stone. I guess the shrug
of his shoulders and an uncomfortable clearing of his throat
was the extent of his interest. Still, I persisted. Showed him slides
of the Matthew triptych, as well as the Martyrdom of Peter
and the Conversion of Paul which got him to admit he wants to read
the Bible again. But that was hardly my point. (I never even got to
the drama of shape or poetry of light.)

Don't get me wrong, we had a good visit; no punches thrown,
subliminally or otherwise. Still, he left me reeling, unable to focus;
maybe even cut, too. I almost went down for the count.
He's been a certain kind of people's champ for a long time. He speaks
their language, plain and simple, shorn of ideals and abstractions.

I can understand. For him, things are only chiaroscuro; negative
shape is silly; black is a color for bad guys ("not saints, for Christ's
sake") and Lord, like the painting of Mary in the Santa Maria del
Popolo, like Mary in every painting, in every church in Rome, saints
are supposed to be ascending to heaven, not crucified upside down
like your Peter singing to the earth or flat on the canvas, eyeless,
under a horse's ass like your Saul.

Look, I'm no fighter, but I'm not going to throw in the towel, either.
Because of you, I see my father in a different light, in a different ring;
the meaning of world has nothing to do with counting, neither
in knockouts nor a percentage of the gate. It is not a matter
of contenders or champs. No doubt, it's a place that needs angels,
though not sitting on clouds with harps watching the forces of good
and evil slug it out. But blue-collar seraphim with double-chins, gray
headed or bald, with bad livers, bad prostates, and, yes, even
bad tempers. Yet, still, bigger than life when fighting for their heretic sons
who write poetry or paint for the sins of the world.

Tuo Amico,
B.

OCTOBER 9
Heart Mountain, WY

Caro Caravaggio,

Today reminds me of you, and those hectic dark days,
your last, on the run, your only rest in the paintings of Matthew.
His revelation of who he was after a lifetime of acting like he knew.
Not the act, the calling, or the angel or even the crucifixion all over
again, but light in and of, around and against the gospel of shapes.
Like today here along the soft edge of the mountain's shadow.
The gray brush of clouds clinging to the bottom of the sky like
giant cobwebs. Only to be blown to bits by a beige wind through
the failing afternoon light. The last of it falling onto lumps of old
sandstone strewn across smallish hills of swollen dirt. Hallowed
autumn in Wyoming like Eden before and after the Fall.

Yet there's something right about it. To sit out here on nothing
but the ground, no more than a nameless weed, wonderfully obscure,
listening to nothing but unseen crickets sing their tick-tock songs of
small black hope. And when the wind dies a little, and still some heat
left in the ghost of day, the last of a brittle light flares up for a moment
in a hundred thousand shards of glass glittering on the basin floor.
Dumb kids, I guess, getting drunk waiting for their calling. I can just
make out in the still thin darkness their tire tracks on the dirt road that's

hardly a road even during the day, winding tentative and reluctant as a last brush stroke after the sun is gone, and the sky still unfinished.

Tuo Amico,
B.

THANKSGIVING

Powell, WY

Carus Juvenal,

I never thought I'd be writing you. I mean I hardly know you.
But my youngest daughter for some mysterious reason picked up
your Satires and won't put them down. I don't know what it is.
She began a little before her birthday in March. Up till then
she was a kind of bubbling optimist who laughed a lot, not very
critical of people or food—like the Romans you criticized,
particularly the aristocracy, who care more for the ambience
than the cuisine.

Not my daughter, no matter if it is plastic bowls, Mickey Mouse
forks and spoons, or one of those awful pink non-spill cups—they're
all fine, better than crystal and chinaware (I mean, what's the fun if
they break every time you happen to drop them?).

Nevertheless, you have become her favorite author, more
than Bert and Ernie's vacation to the woods, more than the Berenstain
Bears, even the Madeline story her older sister likes so much. How
much of a favorite? Well, she reads you not only in translation,
but upside-down! It may have something to do with her changing
world view.

Suddenly out of nowhere a note of selfishness would wail in her tone
to her sister. And her vocabulary had both grown and shrunk by two,
adding the ancient word "Mine!" (Latin, meus) and "No! (non, minime).
I really hope this passes; others have suggested the painful advent
of teeth, or that now because she's gained some independence, or
as you put it, "like some Johnny-come-lately whose feet only yesterday
were white with the chalk (or booties in her case) of the slave-market"
(or bassinet).

Believe me, I don't want to discourage my daughter from reading you.
But, although she relishes your wit as well as I, I think too much
in her case. Just before bed tonight I caught her chewing on your text!
Right on your delicious line attacking the aristocracy, "who deem it
cheaper to feed a lion than a poet," because "poets have bigger
bellies." Ha! Well, it is certainly food for thought or for hungry
daughters. Remember the motto of this day: appetite is all.
Happy Thanksgiving.

Tuus Amicus,
B.

June 19
Spearfish, SD

Carus Virgil,

It's Father's Day over here. A kind of silly idea, wicked
marketing scheme, and harmless custom all rolled into one.
My little ones—two and four—think of it as a day to open presents,
both really hoping there's one for them. My son, who's about the age
of your Aeneas, makes jokes about getting me a tie and some after-
shave. But just a breath below the surface, he is willing to carry me
on his shoulders to hell and back if necessary.

Right now, we're both in different corners of heaven on earth.
Heaven being more a badlands version of the Elysium Fields than any
cathedral paradise with amorphous clouds ringing light. He's over
in Shell, Wyoming, up Trapper Creek. His easel's being soaked with
the "bucolic" life you used to revere. Imagine, Magister, in a shed
with barn swallows for roommates, and not far from the creek, fat
with trout, boasting great leafy cottonwoods.

There's a brood of horses and a goat who thinks he's a horse, but not
nearly as curious, and he could never be a symbol of strength and beauty.
I guess certain medieval types still see the horns and cloven feet
as a kind of life to be avoided. However, my son hasn't said if this goatless
goat is any kind of rural flautist or lover of young girls. We'll see. Oh, and

there's a porcupine too. Gloriously strange creature that somehow makes
a poem of his isolation and reputed ugliness.

Me? Right now, my sacred corner is here along Iron Creek
walled in by the Black Hills with my Dido—red-haired beauty still after
all our journeys. Aeneas missed the boat, I think, not bringing his queen
with him. Perhaps, he wouldn't have taken himself so seriously, wouldn't
have been another walking tragedy. He could have been a poet, instead,
anonymous, always broke, but full of joy and wonder just to be a part
of her epic. *Felix Pater Diem.*

Tuus Amicus,

B.

PONTE SANT' ANGELO, ROME

Above the unholy Tiber on this hallowed bridge
to Saint Peters, Bernini's old bronze angels try
to bless the herds of loud orange buses
bellowing beneath their exhausted wings.
The smudged seraphim avoid looking at them
and at the swarm of tiny cars and scooters
buzzing hell bent to God knows where.
Nor do they gaze heavenward for some
long lost sign out of the blue.

Instead the old host stare hard below
at the ageless water's unwrinkled face,
long undisturbed by the blaring fleets
of loud emperors and deaf popes.
Now bloodless and too slow for sound,
the river flows without flowing,
having been before and after,
asking nothing of the angels above,
but an undamned journey to the sea.

AUGUST 8

Polecat Bench, Wyoming

Caro Bernini,

Nothing in Rome this ruined, not even the Colosseum,
or Constantine in the Campidoglio all broken up in giant pieces
nicely arranged along the walls of the courtyard, but up here
on this spine of bony earth, a jumble of sandstone boulders
haphazard as hell, strewn about without a square in the bunch,
or anything round for that matter, like bad knuckles, a boxer's
or worse, inhuman and calloused like the old ape
in the Sacramento Zoo.

Mean old chimpanzee, ancient, huge, been there probably before
I was born, six by six cage, double fenced, with a tractor tire on a rope
for recreation, alone, ugly, bald-assed from squatting on concrete
all day. A misanthrope who didn't care who knew, spit at people or
threw his shit at them. His last years he wouldn't even do that, sitting
in the far corner by the metal door with his back turned to the few
curious, who still remembered when he would put on a show.

But then no more: hunkered down on his gray haunches
his rubbery chin flattened on his knuckles as if aping Rodin's Thinker.
Somebody's grotesque idea of a joke. He lived past whatever was

supposed to be funny, but not the grotesque like your goofy river men

falling over themselves in the Piazza Navona, trapped

in their fountain with the perfectly ugly church getting the last laugh.

Tuo Amico,

B.

A SMALL ITALIAN RENAISSANCE

(around Bernini's fountain)

Running blindly past one of the falling gods
(the Tigris or Euphrates, it doesn't matter),
a small Roman-eyed boy can't see,
on the verge of crying, but unable to cry,
his mouth open with nothing coming out.

The cry caught in his gargoyled face,
a strangulated plea for mama, for papa,
for anyone who will help his helpless plight.
He freezes in the middle of the piazza.
His grief finally bursts across the stone landscape,
in waves of a wordless need, needing no translation.

His small hand frozen in the warm air,
gestures like Michelangelo's Moses
at the origin in the sky of his deep sorrow:
a balloon, transparent and pink as an angel's wings,
already eclipsing the sun, its string
the last thread to a weeping earth.

Unable to believe anymore (his faith not in things unseen)
he sinks into a large confusion of adults.
Fifteen, twenty, a childhood of minutes later,

he surfaces again out of the swells
of strolling legs and low-slung purses.

His punctured face has healed into a grin too big for him.
Striding to the fountain of foundering gods, he stares
in the pool at his reflection grown closer to heaven:
a new hat anchored to his head.

BERNINI'S FOUNTAIN AT NIGHT

(Piazza Navona)

There's this big broken fingered figure.
He sits damn near falling, perfectly
dry, above the unbroken water
flowing down like crystalline hair.

His heavy back against the thick, black air,
he rides the horseless stone.
It's all he can do, all any of them
marble headed galoots can do,
but balance themselves on the uncertainty
of light.

With his shoulder to the heavy moon,
the swirling crowd threatens to help,
but not for long, as they drift off
to follow their own little stars.

Steering past him, they barely notice
the old God teetering still
from the politics of prayer,
with the emptiest church
forever behind his back.

So, without mariners, what can this water deity do,
but give thanks to his old rock, cut away
from its mother's hard breast so long ago?
His only hope left in his lost index finger,
polished nail and all, gone to simple stone, again.

WRITER'S BLOCK, PIAZZA NAVONA

When I become damned, always
I return to Bernini's fountain,
Here, so many rivers from
Yellowstone where water flows
safely undistinguished,
its salvation untainted
by any Renaissance heroics.

Here, the pigeon marbled fountain,
creekless and crowded, Bernini's
great joke, once loud as the sun,
that nobody hears any more
ringing around the fountain and me
with the latest bits of old Rome.

The tiniest debris I cannot catch,
slipping by so round and fast
I might as well be stone deaf,
not one consonant forms for me
to shape into some gesture of meaning.

The silt of generations builds up and drifts
for hours around the laughing fountain,
and in no time is blown to bits
in the feathery air. I sit, hammerless,
forever drowning in my own thirst.

WHEN THE FOUNTAIN OF FOUR RIVERS FAILS

(Piazza Navona, Rome)

Here, I am hidden from the heat within
the thin shade of this old doorway.
This old iron church door oddly cold
and closed on this hottest Sunday.

Old? What does that mean here
in the middle of the Eternal City
on the end of its latest millennium?

So hot
that most of the black skirted beauties
have gone white print and one more
bodice button unbuttoned (one must
give thanks to all the damn marble saints).

So hot,
with that old water just out of reach
(no swimming in the fountain,
Rome's only law as far as I can tell)
that even Bernini's river men
have fallen into fighting off the sun,
their fat hands and arms all flaying
at the fire and brimstone air.

Against this long-ago side door
invisible in the stone shade
of this quiet dark church,
I attempt a cool distance
from the crowded heat
and this old-as-hell mother of cities.

DECEMBER 30

Powell, WY

Caro Bernini,

I thought of you out of nowhere, the kind of placeless
place certain cold December days are known for, as I watched
a small and unobtrusive sun disappearing over a vague horizon.
More than anything, I remember your angels lining the bridge,
Ponte Sant' Angelo, across the Tiber—dead silent amidst that infernal
noise, those Vespas alone droning like hellish insects from Dante's
humorless Comedy. All that trumpeting humanity ever rolling
roughshod over the edge of their own apocalypse with your angels, stoic
with their blank begrimed eyes somehow a part of it too, watching or
unable to watch. It makes me sigh to think of it, of them, of all that Rome
is or isn't (and it's certainly both): that sacred profane life.

I'm in one of those moods in which I wonder whether it is so
different here. Even now, almost soundless since the sun gave up
the ghost, its final gesture like some last pure note stripped
of its melody lingering atop the head of Heart Mountain. I give up
seeing and listen long into the utterly mute sky, so long
that my listening, itself, grows into a song with no words other
than the barest breeze.

You are a sculptor, you would know the kind of voiceless psalm
that silence sings. It sings of something more than merely another

night crawling out of day's skin. Something more than this quiet cold

with no promise of a round, gold time. It sings of this dead season

that disguises itself in the inertia of stoicism and sacrifice. It sings

a prayer of rest without need of waking, dreamless and beyond

sleep, beyond the restlessness of death, too. It sings like your angels,

the very air smiling and unsmiling as witness to winter's deathless peace.

Tuo Amico,

B.

MILAN

CITY OF LEONARDO

IL DUOMO

In this city of holy commerce another sacred monstrosity
with its busy facade of scenes and characters
from every Biblical story ever told. So many
grotesque busts, statues, and reliefs, you'd think
Hogarth and Breughel had worked here.

A church of fences, corrugated iron
and marble spires puncturing heaven
like small models of the New York skyline.
This, another behemoth of stone faith
which used to prey upon the divine doubt:
old mercantile ancestors, petty bourgeoisie
trembling before the Church's gargantuan sense of itself.

In this noisy morning light, little red and black
cars cruise by with their exhausted faith
in high fashion. While, closest to the street,
Daniel strangles a stone lion: the beast bloodlessly
on its back paws at the traffic of roaring air.

DECEMBER 30
Red Lodge, MT

Caro Leonardo,

Today, signore, we searched for snow. In Red Lodge.
A resort of sorts, though unpretentious by Tahoe or Aspen standards.
Nevertheless, the slopes are draped with spandex, Velcro,
and neon tangerine shapes. We managed our own renaissance,
on a smaller scale, diminutive really, though deserving of a wall
in the Louvre. My girls, masterpieces in plastic sleds of chartreuse
and fuchsia. Down a twenty-foot hill, squealing in their wonder
of snow, and the ecstasy of pure descent made purer with remote
possibilities of danger.

The real risks in their mother's fingers frozen to the video cam,
and my back strain carrying my two-year-old in her pink carnation
suit and her faithful sled up the hill that, truth be told, was no more
than a drawing, a thumbnail sketch in white pencil; worthy of a mural,
of a fresco, but no Last Supper here, no last anything. All firsts
every time, like your blueprints for flight, for a scythed vehicle
and armored car, for hoisting machines, and canal construction,
and all those forays into anatomy, botany, warfare, urban planning,
mechanics, and beauty in the Virgin and Child with St. Anne,
the Virgin of the Rocks, and the Lady with an Ermine.

You could see it in all four-and-a-half years of my daughter, sans sled, sitting down on top of the hill backwards, then pushing off without looking, flat on her back sliding to the bottom red head first (whooping in the blue face of sky): her own version of St. Peter's martyrdom, her descent into the paradise of pure play where there's no distinction between the joyous child and the joy of snow, both mysterious and obvious, in her own world and the furthest circumference of ours. I could feel my dry old wings fluttering every time she became the hill. You would have loved it, Leo, this true melding of science and art, of the oldest truths and the newest beauty, this rebirth of Mona Lisa's smile of smiles spreading forever across my daughters' faces.

Tuo Amico,
B.

LEONARDO'S STATUE (TWO VIEWS)

i

Last night under a cobalt sky, he glared down,
fiercely as Michelangelo's Moses, or worse,
at Milan's upper crust glittering out of La Scala
pearl necked next to black and white tuxedos.
And us, his wayward unknown children's, children's children
committing the great sin below his black gaze:
pencil-less, sans sketch books, not even a blank page,
armed only with the barbaric yawps of our guilt.

ii

Today, halfway paternal (step-father of all
Mona Lisas) as the morning sun
wings about his still solemn shoulders
wrapped in the stone folds of his great cloak.
But, his magnificent hat has become pigeon headed,
the hoary beard like some kind of Christmas wreath
frosts his face that shines the great darkness
of his genius, a masterpiece of stubborn wonder.

JUNE 14
McDonough, GA

Caro Leonardo,

I'm sitting again weeks since at your feet as the La Scala crowd
flooded the piazza spilling a chiaroscuro of pearls and tuxedos,
the color of wealth in any country, paying no heed to us, poor,
(sketch books left at the hotel), artists starving for paper and pencils.
We were indicted by your old cold glare which found us wanting.
"Things will be different," we whined. But I had no idea that here
in the deep South all things are, but in a worse way, if that's possible.

I am still wordless (the pencil a bust) and friendless under
a flowering dogwood unflowering in the greenish heat, the air so thick
you could chisel it into an old dark face full of scorn glaring at
my utter poverty in the worthless shade.

Tuo Amico,
B.

July 12

Migratory Bird Refuge, Bear River, Utah
(For Terry Tempest Williams)

Caro Leonardo,

I know you would like this place. Wild bird refuge.
Of winged silences across broad, flat, liquid nothingness. Nothing
only to our flightless species (no one truly flies in a plane). I'm here
just at the edge of the water where most of them aren't. Unable
to swim or float, I watch in the dim distance great blue herons
and bulky herds of flour colored pelicans. Closer, like sticks stuck
in a mirror, skinny legged, skinny beaked ibises stand
with their translucent green nature hidden in a thin darkness.
They won't let me get too close to really see them, for seeing,
you know, is knowledge and its own kind of flightless flight.

Tuo Amico,

B.

ARCETRI, FLORENCE

HOME OF GALILEO: THE LOST LETTERS

MARCH 2
Cheyenne, WY

Caro Galileo,

It's incredible really, out on Happy Jack Road.
Last night we stopped the car in the blackness—
seven thousand feet up with the lights off.
The moon unplugged just so we could stand
under the forever sunless sky and watch,
sans telescope and mathematically heretical,
the confabulation of a billion stars.
I can't imagine what the Church is going to do
now. You probably didn't get a chance
to hear the radio yesterday, but a couple
of scientists at a convention of astrophysicists
in San Francisco announced that not only one,
but two planets have been discovered somewhere
in the middle of the Milky Way, rolling around
one of those microscopic suns too far to see
with the naked eye. Imagine! The old miracle
happening again and again (as far as we know,
though the Church may think otherwise)—
where a fire smoldering beneath strange soil
burns death to life, melting a tower of ice,

to become moisture in a moment of air, or two....
out there inconceivable! Conception, with or without
a God, it is always divine.

Tuo Amico,
B.

SEPTEMBER 19
Powell, Wyoming

Caro Galileo,

Help! God, I think you're the only soul in the world
who would know what I mean. Last night, it was not much,
even negligible: just this chunky, glob of moon stumbling out
of the sky. Everything too soft, blurred at the edges:
summer ending with a clumsy dance at brightness, more a shuffle
than anything, until gone looking like some sloppy yellowish yoke.

Too many now, maybe then too, might have glanced at it
and shrugged, thinking, we're not talking congressional budget
cuts here, or Middle East peace talks; it's hardly a *People's Magazine*
exclusive, let alone *The National Enquirer* (I can almost hear
their irritation), so what's the big deal?

Ok, the moon, a lonely late thing, but that's common enough stuff,
and after it's over, what's left? A lot of black nothing to bank on,
utterly uneventful even peppered with a couple dozen dim stars.
But, Signore Galilei, I watched it, nevertheless, until my eyes fell
like soft rain, until I heard my still too young daughter's breathing
and heard, too, the earth, half humming, half silent in a wholly
unfathomable way that only you would understand.

Tuo Amico,

B.

JULY 16

Powell, WY

Caro Galileo,

Tonight, God, unbelievable, Jupiter is being smashed into
by a comet. All I've got is some cheap binoculars and a pair
of weakening naked eyes. I don't know what to believe or think.
NASA, or whoever oversees space watching these days,
has all kinds of powerful telescopes, fifty to a thousand times better
than yours, including one, the Hubble, circling the earth. And They
don't know either what will happen.

Ironic isn't it that the They of the seventeenth century threw you,
an old man of seventy, into prison, threatened your family and who
knows what else with intimidation because you saw that true belief is not
in things unseen. I'm not so sure. So, I stepped outside tonight late,
so very late under Wyoming's sacred black sky with more stars
than angels in paradise.

 I looked toward the giant planet, still the biggest in our modest
corner of a curved heaven. And looking at that unwavering pin
of light, I could feel the pulse of the earth quicken and something
tremble in my blood. It seemed each intertwined into a rhythm of truth
beyond any optics, subtler, interior, and invisible yet somehow
vaster than all cosmologies. I don't know how to prove it, neither

in theory nor scientific experiments, not even through any genuine articles of faith, but I know the truth of the universe is orbiting within the spheres of my heart.

Tuo Amico,

B.

July 18

Powell, WY

Caro Galileo,

I know I said I'd write every day the fragments of the comet
struck Jupiter. But we've had our own collisions. Daycare ended
last Friday and our babysitter left on vacation and yesterday mi amico
Giovanni and his family with our beautiful Tuscan "cousins" were here
for barbecued salmon. We all watched the world cup soccer
championship game between Italia and Brasilia. Alas, the South
Americans won by one penalty kick: Gianluca Fabiani, fifteen and full
of the old and new worlds, was crushed; Sylvia, his sister and a shoulder
strap away from Diana (si, signore, the Diana), was only slightly wounded.
Suddenly, I found myself disliking Brazil, a country about which I know
next to nothing except that they can play soccer better than anyone else in
the world.

I think differences between people, like that of the planets,
should be left up to specialists who speak about such things in ways
that no laymen could ever understand. For me, the idea of difference
has always been the straw—the only one, thin and dry as nothing—
that breaks all worlds' back time and again. I was reminded of this
today when another huge fragment, the largest of them all, crashed
into the planet and Jupiter became its own sun, momentarily.
You know astrologers (yes, they're still around) say Jupiter, among

other things, is the planet of jollity, and tonight it laughed into a brightness beyond any cosmic jokes. In no need of its moons, or that remote, indifferent sun, Jupiter became what we so desperately need: its own Otherness, a light unto itself.

Tuo Amico,
B.

JULY 19
Powell, WY

Caro Galileo,

I'm not sure if I feel closer or farther away from you, from Florence,
from Italy tonight. I'm not sure if it is a night for feeling anything. Not
the clear-cut emotion needed for matters of gravity or weightlessness.
So, I drink gin. It's summer, what the hell. And another day
of bombardments. Jupiter. Seven more pieces of that infernal comet
slamming into the great planet's already dark side. And here Rwanda
is the latest heresy, and in Argentina a Jewish embassy bombed,
and on the Gaza strip an Israeli soldier was shot in the head.

"The comet was not a dud," claimed one scientist. Maybe all
the explosions on Jupiter will transfigure the energy here?
The immeasurable kind, which webs and nets and glazes over all
the cracks of the universe. You know, there has not been any water
vapor released into the Jovian atmosphere when each fragment hit,
like they expected. No water on Jupiter, just like in Wyoming,
and like in all the hearts of the terrorists who think they are
their own little planets somehow disconnected from the rest
of the solar system. Maybe the shock waves from Jupiter will
knock every hate-monger down, and during their fall they will
see what you discovered a long time ago, how everyone returns
to mother earth the same way.

Tuo Amico,

B.

JULY 21
Powell, WY

Caro Galileo,

Sorry I couldn't write last night. Three comet fragments
struck Jupiter, one right after the other. Scientists joked about
the "triple whammy," but there's a crater the size of the earth out
of which pours plumes of some terrible kind of smoke. Everybody
is so happy, from astrophysicist to amateur astronomer, laughing,
back-slapping each other, and beaming into the blank eye
of the camera. Congratulations are in order, they say, because
they are seeing this galactic "show" for the first time. Five years
ago, a meteor a mile wide missed the earth by six hours;
they didn't see that until after it hurtled by.

But last night, I couldn't write because I felt so far away from
the ground. It was the 25th anniversary of the first man on the moon.
I felt cheated back then, because I felt the moon had been robbed
of its mystery, a rape of Diana with an entire mob cheering across
the country. I'm writing now because I'm not angry anymore.
I understand now the power of the moon, its poetry and magic
are greater than any footprints in the sand.

Here, today, it's 93 degrees Fahrenheit, full sunlight, a classic
summer day. Yesterday's pessimism, fatalism, and cowardice

have no place in the world today. I watch my children run in circles,

orbiting each other—earth and moon, moon and earth, their bright

laughter more powerful than ten thousand comets slamming

into me. I feel like congratulating myself, because I can see this

so clearly. Perception has made me big again, and, like Jupiter,

I am my own light.

Tuo Amico,

B.

APRIL 12
Powell, WY

Caro Galileo,

Two years ago, I thought there was nothing more to say.
The gulf between your knowledge of God knows everything
and my great lack was too much. As the French say, I wanted to
engagé your mind. Not simply chat over the backyard fence about
the weather or the latest spring fashions, or how the gli Azzurri,
your National Football Team or my Colorado Rockies are doing.
But to engagé, immerse ourselves in the phenomenal workings
of the world: for you, how things move, down or up or around,
the perception of which becomes knowledge, becomes a movement
in us; for me, my ignorance intact, it wasn't how or what or even why
something moved, but the moving itself, to move with that Other:
that boulder being catapulted, that melon plummeting to
the cobblestone, that earth whirling dervish around the sun.
You see now why my letters stopped.
I didn't want to annoy you with my frenetic naiveté.

Then this new comet, Hyakutake, not striking Jupiter, but
coming so close to the earth, the whole world began running
to the edge of the horizon to watch. Everyone saw it, my mother strolling
through the Californian twilight, my brother working late outside of
a Seattle post office, even deep in the Georgia woods my sister-in-law

pulling ticks off her dog. But not me. Both a week before and every day
of its brightest week, I had bragged that sitting in a lawn chair at five
thousand feet above sea level, no one would see it better. I took my time,
didn't get excited: me the luckiest hare and that tortoise comet.

But I forgot. This is Wyoming. Where winter lingers far longer
than anywhere else, heavy with all of its self-importance, its staying power
like an old goat, its gray beard full of snow, so no sky, not even a scratch
of moon across one black moment, one damn night. So, I gave up and
watched ABC's Nightline special on the comet with all the experts and
all the amateurs and all the odd people who had never even seen a star
before, who boasted of being hypnotized by
the spectacle for a whole hour. Even Hyakutake himself, blazing
with pride, his finger in the inky vastness, pointing out "his" comet.

Then Monday, I don't know how, but spring showed up a month
late, looking not much like Botticelli's painting, more bone than flesh,
sans torch colored hair, this bald Primavera. Yet, I was inspired out into
the pure blackness to stare at one anonymous constellation after another
all over the starry heavens. Hell, I couldn't even find the Big Dipper.
All over again, I could feel the gulf widening between your world
and mine. I began to cave in. What was the point of a comet anyway?
Some kind of frozen ball of gas burning itself up across the universe
is not much different from many hot aired souls down here,
myself included. Oh, not you, Signore Galilei, despite how much
your great light blinded me standing there emptied, uninspired,
lightless in the mid-orbit of my life.

And then, can you imagine! I quit looking at the sky. The silence
rung around me like a choir of obsolete seraphim. I listened to nothing,
but the echoes of my last hollow thoughts, growing bleaker than the black
above. Suddenly, skinny sounds began in the southeast over the scalped,
homely McCullough Peaks where stocky wild horses scamper across
fossilized turtle shells and saber-tooth tiger scat five miles full
of emptiness from my house.

I think you'd recognize this noise, not quite metallic, neither
a clanging or steel ringing, nor enough brass to trumpet or trombone.
More like sad clarinets, blowing single notes,
only a couple at first, bleating
high c and low, major and minor, tuneless really, until more, forty, fifty,
an entire orchestra of mad clarinets. There was no telling and no seeing
either, just a cacophony of honking headed in my direction. Yes, by God,
geese, branta canadensis, Canadian honkers. Hallelujah!
Finally, something concrete. No damn gaseous ball, but birds, big
with loud wings who would be directly overhead in seconds, and low
enough, I hoped, for me to touch a weathered feather, or a webbed foot,
still wet. I longed to behold their bulky grace,
and feel their aching chorus rain down on me.

I waited listening to the sky shrink a hundred yards, fifty, thirty,
to where the houses perch on the edge of the bluff, then just at the peak
of my roof, just fifteen geese wings from me, they stopped, in mid-air,
singing, crying, calling, honking, chanting, as if by magic or some pre-

arranged signal; they had fallen into a mass of silence. Only the air being swept by a hundred invisible brooms into a pile of feathery wind, blown about my head, my hair flung into the ineffable goose sky.

The entire flock honed into arrow consciousness, thinking itself
northwest across the lunar space of Badger Basin toward and over
the hulking Beartooth Mountains, following some aerial Going-to-the-
Sun Road over Glacier Park, and into Canada, past Kootenay and Banff,
further on straight up the Meander River into the Northwest Territories
becoming holy geese on pilgrimage to their ancestral waters,
the Beaufort Sea, to Banks Island, Melville Island,
and, at last, to Bathurst, home
to these polar spirits alighting atop the world.

Only then, my dear Galileo, did I see why they had come,
these raucous souls, how their whole sound had been aimed at that
eggless egg falling slowly in the far night sky, the rush of their wings
chanting there, there, there: unmistakable Hyakutake,
its comet tail strewn like pieces of shell. Dull and fuzzy. You'd laugh at
this, but it shocked me into speechless awe, this coldest ball of cosmic
dust gassing its way through space, earthless, airless, the furthest thing
from all tangible life, utterly godless.

Yet these geese knew, these souls of habitual flight, whose instinct is the
nature of all orbits, knew this comet as a piece of the primordial puzzle.
Its mere presence, suddenly I knew, was all the evidence
the Church Fathers or your faithless descendants needed of an Unmoved

Mover—brooding upon the deep or Big Bang or both—the origin of all motion, the bridging of all gulfs of time, of space, of life and death, of you and me. So, we can say, together, honking each to each, alone, tat tvam asi, thou are that, too.

Tuo Amico,
B.

ABOUT THE AUTHOR

Burt Bradley lived on a bluff in Northwest Wyoming seventy miles from Yellowstone National Park for over thirty years, with his wife Janet, a photographer. He devoted his life to delving into the wild serenity of the greater Yellowstone ecosystem. His writing has appeared in *Ring of Fire: Writers of the Yellowstone Region, Michigan Quarterly Review, Best of Writers at Work*, among others. He served as a professor emeritus at Northwest College in Powell, Wyoming, where he taught Writing in the Wild classes in Yellowstone and the Southwest Desert. His first collection, *After Following*, won the Homebound Publications Poetry Prize in 2018. *Letters to Michelangelo from Wyoming* is his second full-length work. Sadly, he continued his journey on before seeing it released, but lived the words in these pages to the fullest.

For more information on Burt Bradley's work and legacy visit:
WWW.HOMEBOUNDPUBLICATIONS.COM

HOMEBOUND
PUBLICATIONS

We are an award-winning independent publisher founded in 2011 striving to ensure that the mainstream is not the only stream. More than a company, we are a community of writers and readers exploring the larger questions we face as a global village. It is our intention to preserve contemplative storytelling. We publish full-length introspective works of creative non-fiction, literary fiction, and poetry. *Fly with us into our 10th year.*

WWW.HOMEBOUNDPUBLICATIONS.COM

CPSIA information can be obtained
at www.ICGtesting.com
Printed in the USA
JSHW040713060421
13270JS00007B/24